DING-DONG,
THE WITCH IS DEAD

DING-DONG, THE WITCH IS DEAD

Prophet
Walter Wilkins

ISBN: 979-8-9871048-0-4 – Paperback
eISBN: 979-8-9871048-1-1 – Ebook

1 1 0 9 2 2

Library of Congress Control Number: 2022918649

♾This paper meets the requirements of ANSI/NISO Z39.48-1992 (Permanence of Paper)

Author Photo by Williams Photography

In remembrance of my dear sister,
Penny Wilkins

Acknowledgments

I would like to thank God for my dear mother, Holly Wilkins, who always believed in me and inspired me to do what God had called me to do.

CONTENTS

INTRODUCTION

Ring the bell and sound the alarm: witchcraft is real! There are far too many people who simply do not believe that witchcraft is real and that witchcraft is spoken about in the Bible. Oftentimes, they think there is something wrong with people who do believe in witchcraft because they are aware of the facts concerning witchcraft.

In this book, *Ding-Dong, the Witch Is Dead*, I will share personal stories of how I became possessed by a witch spirit and how it almost destroyed my life and the lives of others. You will also learn information on what a witch is and what witchcraft is, as well as be enlightened on how we can become possessed by witchcraft.

Generally, we think that witchcraft is something that others put on, such as a curse or a spell. However, we can also become possessed by a witch spirit through our own sins. The devil then literally possesses us—we have a witch spirit. The witch spirit causes us to create havoc, chaos, confusion, wickedness, and more on the lives of others and ourselves.

The good news, and my hope, is that after reading my book you will have the knowledge of how witchcraft can be broken and stopped forever.

Ring the bell and sound the alarm: Ding-Dong, the Witch Is Dead!

PART ONE

DING-DONG, WITCHCRAFT IS REAL

CHAPTER ONE

POWER TO CAST OUT A WITCH

"For God hath not given us the spirit of fear;
but of power, and of love, and of a sound mind"
(2 Timothy 1:7 (KJV)).

The number twelve is a very significant number in the Bible. The number twelve is considered a perfect number that symbolizes God's power, authority, and completeness. Luke 2:42 records, **"When he [Jesus] was twelve years old, they went up to the festival, according to the custom"** (NIV).

"Everyone who heard him was amazed . . ." *(Luke 2:47 (NIV)).*

It was at the age of twelve that I heard the voice of God speaking to me. The Lord was calling me into the gospel ministry of preaching and deliverance. God was saving me from a worldly life. The primary reason the Lord wanted me saved was to use me to save others in a world of sin.

After many lengthy, heartfelt conversations with my pastor about what I had heard God say, my pastor said he wanted to assist God in using me by preparing me to do God's work. The pastor said the first step was to baptize me. Shortly after being baptized by my pastor, Jesus baptized me with the power of the Holy Ghost, and the Spirit of the Lord according to the Gospel of Luke came upon me: "*The Spirit of the Lord is upon me, because he hath anointed me to preach the gospel to the poor; he hath sent me to heal the brokenhearted, to preach deliverance to the captives, and recovering of sight to the blind, to set at liberty them that are bruised, To preach the acceptable year of the Lord*" **(Luke 4:18–19 (KJV)).**

I soon started preaching with power, might, strength, and wisdom that could only come from the Most High God. People would pack the church to see the boy preacher that the Lord was using in such a mighty way. Initially, people came as spectators to see me, but then they started coming to hear the True Word of God, to witness and experience the power of God as God used me to perform miracles, signs, and wonders! People would ponder with disbelief, excitement, and inquisitiveness over how God could use a mere boy, who did not have much life experience to preach, prophesy, heal, and deliver people!

Each time I stood before the people in church services, my family, friends, even the pastors, would always be in awe. Amazed because God was using me, a child, to bless them all in such a powerful and enormously unprecedented manner with prophetic

4

words and amazing miracles! I, too, marvel and shudder as I think about how God used me at such an early time in my life to operate in such a powerful way.

Yes, God used me to heal people from all types of ailments and diseases: cancer, AIDS, diabetes, sickle cell, lupus, arthritis, and more. God's power even empowered people in wheelchairs to walk. The Lord also used me to cast spirits of depression, suicide, substance addiction, as well as demonic spirits and witchcraft, out of people. In services, whenever I started walking behind the church pews, I knew the power of God was resting upon me in a powerful way! At that point, I knew the Lord had fully taken over me.

I can recall one of those occasions like it was yesterday: At that time, I was fourteen years old. I was at an evening church service ministering to the glory of God like I was a grown man. After preaching, the Lord told me to start ministering to the people. As young as I was, I could hear the voice of God with clarity and accuracy. The people were excited and so was I as God started using me to prophesy to the congregation.

In one of the services, there was a woman sitting in the center pew, in the center section of the church. As I stood in the pulpit, I had a bird's-eye view of her. This woman never took her eyes off me as she looked at me with an intense glaring glare.

While I was preaching, I noticed her squirming in her seat; she was extremely uncomfortable as I delivered the Word of God. This woman became even more uneasy and tense once God started using me in the deliverance service in a mighty way. God gave me a special word for many people and to several people sitting near this woman—but not to her. She became even more agitated, now almost to the point of being irritated and angry. Her eyes started to shift as they changed to a fiery red and blazed at me.

Now, I must admit she did make me feel a little timid, yet God kept speaking to me, giving me messages for various people in the church and telling me, "Son, do not fear—I am with you and I will protect you." I pushed fear out of my mind and focused on hearing the voice of God that was empowering me to deliver his people from being imprisoned and held captive by the devil. I refused to allow my fear and lack of experience in this type of deliverance to stop the Lord from using me!

It was as if the demonic spirit in her overheard the conversation between God and myself, because this woman immediately came out into the aisle toward me. Her body started to flinch, sway, as it transformed in a disfigured manner right before my eyes. It startled me greatly, and if I can be honest, it scared me. But then I heard God with a thunderous voice in my ear saying, "Don't you move, don't you step back, nor withdraw." God said, "I've got this!"

It was at this point that I felt the Lord taking over my being, as I moved toward this witch without any fear because I knew God was in complete control—not the boy preacher, not Walter, but the Power of Jesus!

The witch demon in this woman caused her to fall to the floor as God spoke directly to her. The witch in her started squirming and crawling on the floor of the church like a snake, as she foamed from the mouth, making ungodly sounds.

God continued to speak through me as I cast the witch out of her. I could not see anyone else, only this thing, the witch in the woman emerging, making strange noises, and the voice of God coming from within me.

I can only imagine how frightened the people were, too scared to move and too captivated by what they were seeing to mumble a word or make a sound. This was only the beginning of God using me to cast the witch demons and witchcraft out of people.

CHAPTER TWO

WITCHCRAFT IS REAL . . .

"Let no one be found among you who sacrifices their son or daughter in the fire, who practices divination or sorcery, interprets omens, engages in witchcraft, or casts spells" (Deuteronomy 18:10–11 (NIV)).

WHAT IS A WITCH?

A witch is considered to be a person who practices witchcraft. When most people think about a witch, they often envision the witch costume that is popular to wear during Halloween. Others may think about the portrait of the witch from the popular 1939 film, *The Wizard of Oz*. In the movie, the evil Wicked Witch of the West is a woman with a long, narrow, and warty nose, dressed in all black, and wearing a wide-brimmed, black, pointed hat. She rides on a broom, her mouth wide open as she laughs a wicked laugh, seeking someone to cast a spell on—"witchcraft."

Fairy tales and children's books often witches as antagonist characters. The antagonist witch, usually places a spell, curse, or potion upon the primary character which alters their lives in a negative manner. Stories such as *Rapunzel, Snow White, Sleeping Beauty, Room on the Broom, It's Raining Bats & Frogs, Beauty and the Beast,* and *The Little Mermaid* to name a few. Without a doubt, the most famous fairy tale to feature a witch as the main adversary, *Hansel & Gretel* follows the adventures of the two siblings after they are abandoned in an enchanted forest by their parents and encounters a witch. *The Princess and the Frog* is noted as being a globally popular fairy-tale movie that carries a wonderful moral—to accept everyone regardless of their looks—but the story is about a prince who is cursed by a witch and turned into a frog.

Once upon a time, as I evangelized in a church service, I encountered a man who testified that a woman had had a witch cast a spell on him. He said that he knew it had occurred when he no longer felt or acted like his normal self. This man stated that he was no longer in control of himself, doing and saying things to others that he would not normally do. One of his primary concerns had to do with his love life. The woman he loved was not the woman he was with and the woman he was with was not the one he wanted to be with, but he simply could not control himself.

On this particular Sunday evening, he said he had to really force and fight with himself to get to the church service. He desperately desired to get to church, because he had heard that the guest preacher had the power to break witchcraft spells on people. This man said it was as if there were two people, one good and one bad, inside of him; the two were constantly tugging with each other.

That Sunday as I stood in the pulpit, I noticed this man flinching and rocking back and forth. Then, all of a sudden, he charged the pulpit, placing his hands around my neck, choking the life out of me. I could not breathe. He was literally trying with all his might to kill me! As others tried to get him off me, I started praying, rebuking, pleading the blood of Jesus, and calling the devil—the witch spirit in him—out. As this "thing" inside of him came out, he screamed, cried, and squirmed on the floor, losing his grip from my neck and falling to the floor.

WHAT IS WITCHCRAFT?

Merriam-Webster Dictionary defines witchcraft as "the use of sorcery or magic; communication with the devil or with a familiar; an irresistible influence or fascination; rituals and practices that incorporate belief in magic and that are associated especially with neo-pagan traditions and religions (such as Wicca)."

Those who practice Wicca as a religion, practice witchcraft. They use tools such as the broom as a purifying symbol, the wand, candles, crystals and the knife. *Encyclopedia Britannica* says that Wicca is a "modern Western witchcraft movement that is very popular today. Some practitioners consider Wicca the religion of pre-Christian Europe, forced underground by the Christian church ... Wicca focuses on the goddess as the supreme being and usually excludes men. Wiccans share a belief in the importance of the feminine principle, a deep respect for nature, and a pantheistic and polytheistic worldview."

If you are not familiar with this topic, then use this as an introduction to what witchcraft is and why you must guard against it. You will discover that you can be infected by this in ways you may not think about. No matter what time period or culture, witchcraft has always been the same.

The actions of witchcraft are carried out by manipulation (control) and spiritual means.

A. Manipulation – This is all about influence, usually in an unfair manner. People who manipulate others attack their mental and emotional sides to get what they want.

Manipulation is not good, nor does it make the victim feel good, whether it's by a friend, family member, or partner. In order to keep from being victimized by a manipulator—a witch—it is vital to know the signs of a manipulation. Some of the signs include:

1. They guilt trip you.
2. They ignore your input.
3. They don't give you time to make decisions.
4. They don't help you resolve problems.
5. They undermine your self-confidence.
6. They force you out of your comfort zone.

7. They butter you up with small requests.
8. They pretend to be concerned.
9. They intentionally disregard you.
10. They offer you the silent treatment.
11. They behave passive-aggressively.
12. They withhold things from you.
13. They wear you down.

B. Spiritual Means – When you call on assistance that steps outside of your realm of ability. In the case of spiritists and mediums, this is demonic assistance.

"There shall not be found among you any one that maketh his son or his daughter to pass through the fire, or that useth divination, or an observer of times, or an enchanter, or a witch. Or a charmer, or a consulter with familiar spirits, or a wizard, or a necromancer. For all that do these things are an abomination unto the Lord: and because of these abominations the Lord thy God doth drive them out from before thee" (Deuteronomy 18:10–12 (KJV)).

When you put it all together, witchcraft is trying to insert influence and control with demonic assistance into a situation. Witchcraft is often used by one person to try to control another person.

Witchcraft is dangerous and not of God. Even our God, who is our creator, does not try to control us. God gives us a free will. We are free to choose to live our lives in a manner that is pleasing to God, or we can choose to live our lives the way we want to; it is our choice. This is the danger of witchcraft, because the person makes the choice to live life the way they choose and, with the aid of witchcraft, choose to control the lives of others.

Witchcraft was present during biblical times and throughout history and continues to influence our cultures of today. We don't always recognize it for what it is because it is not always apparent, and is, oftentimes, disguised as something else, such as manipulation. Yet we need to be on guard and sound the alarm concerning what the Bible says about witchcraft.

CHAPTER THREE

THE BIBLE SAYS WITCHCRAFT IS . . .

"I will destroy your witchcraft and you will no longer cast spells" (Micah 5:12 (NIV)).

Throughout the Bible, in both the Old and New Testament writings, we find scriptures giving reference to witches and witchcraft. Psalm 59, written by King David, is interpreted by some as a psalm about a witch, witchcraft, and the power of evil attacking David prior to his becoming king.

"Deliver me from my enemies, O God;
*   be my fortress against those who are*
*   attacking me.*
Deliver me from evildoers
*   and save me from those who are after my*
*   blood.*
See how they lie in wait for me!

Fierce men conspire against me
for no offense or sin of mine, Lord.
I have done no wrong, yet they are ready
to attack me.
Arise to help me; look on my plight!
You, Lord God Almighty,
you who are the God of Israel,
rouse yourself to punish all the nations;
show no mercy to wicked traitors.
They return at evening,
snarling like dogs,
and prowl about the city.
See what they spew from their mouths —
the words from their lips are sharp as
swords, and they think, 'Who can hear us?'
But you laugh at them, Lord;
you scoff at all those nations.
You are my strength, I watch for you;
you, God, are my fortress,
my God on whom I can rely.
God will go before me
and will let me gloat over those who
slander me.
But do not kill them, Lord our shield,
or my people will forget.
In your might uproot them
and bring them down.
For the sins of their mouths,
for the words of their lips,
let them be caught in their pride.
For the curses and lies they utter,

> *consume them in your wrath,*
> *consume them till they are no more.*
> *Then it will be known to the ends of the earth*
> *that God rules over Jacob.*
> *They return at evening,*
> *snarling like dogs,*
> *and prowl about the city.*
> *They wander about for food*
> *and howl if not satisfied.*
> *But I will sing of your strength,*
> *in the morning I will sing of your love;*
> *for you are my fortress,*
> *my refuge in times of trouble.*
> *You are my strength, I sing praise to you;*
> *you, God, are my fortress,*
> *my God on whom I can rely"*
> **(Psalm 59 (NIV)).**

King Saul had taken on a destructive spirit of re-bellion caused by his jealousy and hatred of his armor bearer David. David was handsome, kind, caring, gifted, fearless, and anointed and appointed by God to replace Saul as king. All of this threatened Saul, which led to rebellion and opened the portal for the "witch spirit" to possess him (I will talk more about this later). *"Saul died because he was unfaithful to the Lord; he did not keep the word of the Lord and even consulted a medium for guidance"* **(1 Chronicles 10:13).**

Please note that in this psalm, David prayed vigor-ously that God would deliver him from the hands of his enemy. God was faithful throughout all of David's struggles caused by Saul. The story ends with Saul's death and David becoming king of Israel. The verses of 1 Chronicles 10:13–14 (NIV) tell us, *"Saul died because he was unfaithful to the Lord; he did not keep the word of the Lord and even consulted a medium for guidance, and did not inquire of the Lord. So the Lord put him to death and turned the kingdom over to David son of Jesse."*

It is also true for each of us that no matter what the enemy tries to do to us, when you intentionally seek God, God will give you the victory. In this prayer, David teaches us three valuable things. First, to acknowledge our problem and pray. Second, we must take on a prophetic spirit of hopefulness. The hope in knowing that if we seek God, our current situation will not remain the same. Third, to have the confidence that the grace of God will deliver us from our enemies.

God is informing us in Deuteronomy 18:10–12 that these things are evil, idolatrous, and are demonic spirits. They are all abominations to God. We should not get involved in anything that will cause the wrath and destruction of God to come upon us.

The Bible tells us in Leviticus 20:6 (NIV), *"I will set my face against anyone who turns to mediums and spiritists to prostitute themselves by following them, and I will cut them off from their people."* To God, seeking counseling from mediums and spiritists is compared to seeking to have sex with a prostitute, which is a spiritual immorality. God also compares the spiritual sin of witchcraft to the physical sins of prostitution. When a man or woman visits a prostitute, they create harm in their relationship with their spouse or significant other. The spiritual and physical sins are both an abomination to God. God wants us to keep our lives holy. The Apostle Paul writes in 2 Corinthians 7:1 (NIV), *"Therefore, since we have these promises, dear friends, let us purify ourselves from everything that contaminates body and spirit, perfecting holiness out of reverence for God."*

The New Testament teaches against *"the acts of the flesh; sexual immorality, impurity and debauchery; idolatry and witchcraft; hatred, discord, jealousy, fits of rage, selfish ambition, dissensions, factions, envy; drunkenness, orgies, and the like. 'I warn you, as I did before, that those who live like this will not inherit the kingdom of God'"* **(Galatians 5:19–21).** The sexual sins, which are physical sins, are listed in verse 19 of the King James Version as adultery, fornication, immorality, impurity, and debauchery. Followed by the names of the spiritual sins idolatry and witchcraft in verse 20. Those who live by the flesh in physical, spiritual, or any of the other sins listed, will not inherit The Kingdom of God, as told by the Apostle Paul.

Below are fourteen powerful Scriptural references on witchcraft and the spirit of a witch:

1. *"Saul died because he was unfaithful to the LORD; he did not keep the word of the LORD and even consulted a medium for guidance"* (1 Chronicles 10:13 (NIV)).

2. *"For rebellion is like the sin of divination, and arrogance like the evil of idolatry. Because*

you have rejected the word of the LORD, he has rejected you as king" (1 Samuel 15:23 (NIV)).

3. *"He sacrificed his children in the fire in the Valley of Ben Hinnom, practiced divination and witchcraft, sought omens, and consulted mediums and spiritists. He did much evil in the eyes of the LORD, arousing his anger"* (2 Chronicles 33:6 (NIV)).

4. *"Do not turn to mediums or seek out spiritists, for you will be defiled by them. I am the LORD your God" (Leviticus 19:31).*

5. *"A man or woman who is a medium or spiritist among you must be put to death. You are to stone them; their blood will be on their own heads'"* (Leviticus 20:27 (NIV)).

6. *"The light of a lamp will never shine in you again. The voice of bridegroom and bride will never be heard in you again. Your merchants were the world's important people. By your magic spell all the nations were led astray"* (Revelation 18:23 (NIV))

7. *"But the cowardly, the unbelieving, the vile, the murderers, the sexually immoral, those who practice magic arts, the idolaters and all liars—they will be consigned to the fiery lake of burning sulfur. This is the second death"* (Revelations 21:8 (NIV)).

8. *"The acts of the flesh are obvious: sexual immorality, impurity and debauchery; 20*

idolatry and witchcraft; hatred, discord, jealousy, fits of rage, selfish ambition, dissensions, factions 21 and envy; drunkenness, orgies, and the like. I warn you, as I did before, that those who live like this will not inherit the kingdom of God" (Galatians 5:19–20 (NIV)).

9. *"When this became known to the Jews and Greeks living in Ephesus, they were all seized with fear, and the name of the Lord Jesus was held in high honor. Many of those who believed now came and openly confessed what they had done. A number who had practiced sorcery brought their scrolls together and burned them publicly. When they calculated the value of the scrolls, the total came to fifty thousand drachmas. In this way the word of the Lord spread widely and grew in power"* (Acts 19:17–20 (NIV)).

10. *"When someone tells you to consult mediums and spiritists, who whisper and mutter, should not a people inquire of their God? Why consult the dead on behalf of the living? Consult God's instruction and the testimony of warning. If anyone does not speak according to this word, they have no light of dawn. Distressed and hungry, they will roam through the land; when they are famished, they will become enraged and, looking upward, will curse their king and their God. Then they will look toward the*

earth and see only distress and darkness and fearful gloom, and they will be thrust into utter darkness" (Isaiah 8:19–22 (NIV)).

11. *"'Give me also this ability so that everyone on whom I lay my hands may receive the Holy Spirit.' Peter answered: 'May your money perish with you, because you thought you could buy the gift of God with money! You have no part or share in this ministry, because your heart is not right before God. Repent of this wickedness and pray to the Lord in the hope that he may forgive you for having such a thought in your heart. For I see that you are full of bitterness and captive to sin'"* (Acts 8:19–23 (NIV)).

12. *"A prophecy against Egypt: See, the LORD rides on a swift cloud and is coming to Egypt. The idols of Egypt tremble before him, and the hearts of the Egyptians melt with fear. "I will stir up Egyptian against Egyptian—brother will fight against brother, neighbor against neighbor, city against city, kingdom against kingdom. The Egyptians will lose heart, and I will bring their plans to nothing; they will con-sult the idols and the spirits of the dead, the mediums and the spiritists. I will hand the Egyptians over to the power of a cruel master, and a fierce king will rule over them," declares the Lord, the LORD Almighty"* (Isaiah 19:1–4 (NIV)).

13. *"Let no one be found among you who sacrifices their son or daughter in the fire, who practices divination or sorcery, interprets omens, engages in witchcraft, or casts spells, or who is a medium or spiritist or who consults the dead. Anyone who does these things is detestable to the LORD; because of these same detestable practices the LORD your God will drive out those nations before you. You must be blameless before the LORD your God. The nations you will dispossess listen to those who practice sorcery or divination. But as for you, the LORD your God has not permitted you to do so"* (Deuteronomy 18:10–14 (NIV)).

14. *"Now then, listen, you lover of pleasure, lounging in your security and saying to yourself, 'I am, and there is none besides me. I will never be a widow or suffer the loss of children.' Both of these will overtake you in a moment, on a single day: loss of children and widowhood. They will come upon you in full measure, in spite of your many sorceries and all your potent spells. You have trusted in your wickedness and have said, 'No one sees me.' Your wisdom and knowledge mislead you when you say to yourself, 'I am, and there is none besides me.' Disaster will come upon you, and you will not know how to conjure it away. A calamity will fall upon*

23

you that you cannot ward off with a ransom; a catastrophe you cannot foresee will suddenly come upon you. "Keep on, then, with your magic spells and with your many sorceries, which you have labored at since childhood. Perhaps you will succeed, perhaps you will cause terror. All the counsel you have received has only worn you out! Let your astrologers come forward, those stargazers who make predictions month by month, let them save you from what is coming upon you. Surely they are like stubble; the fire will burn them up. They cannot even save themselves from the power of flame. These are not coals for warmth; this is not a fire to sit by" (Isaiah 47:8–14 (NIV)).

PART TWO

THE DINGS AND DONGS OF WITCHCRAFT

Chapter Four

Witchcraft Destroys

"The thief comes only to steal and kill and destroy; I have come that they may have life, and have it to the full" (John 10:10 (NIV)).

Witchcraft is **dangerous, divisive, and destructive**; it has always sought to control the lives of others, which ultimately destroys them. Witchcraft was present during biblical times, throughout history, and continues to influence our cultures of today. We don't always recognize it for what it is, because it is not always apparent, and is oftentimes disguised as something else. Yet we need to be on guard and sound the alarm concerning what the Bible says about witchcraft.

WITCHCRAFT IS DANGEROUS

The Bible is very clear about its position on witchcraft, and you will find many warnings in the scriptures about the danger and about the importance of staying away from it. In Leviticus 19:26, we are told, ***"Do not practice divination or seek omens"*** **(NIV)**.

When you put this together, witchcraft is trying to insert influence and control with demonic assistance into a situation. Witchcraft is often used by one person to try to control another person. Witchcraft is dangerous and not of God.

God's opinion about these things is quite evident—they are detestable to him. In case you were wondering, the word "detestable" can also mean abomination. God hates those detestable actions.

WITCHCRAFT IS DIVISIVE

In the Bible, God gives strong warnings to stay far away from witchcraft. God told the people of Israel, ***"Do not turn to mediums or seek out spiritists, for you will be defiled by them. I am the Lord your God"*** **(Leviticus 19:31 (NIV))**.

In some biblical translations the word "sorcery" is used instead of witchcraft. Sorcery in Greek comes from the word *"Pharmakeia"*—the words "pharmacy" and "pharmaceutical" are derived from it. Witches and sorcerers use drugs and other potions to put on people "in spirit" so their magic will work.

Mediums or spiritists will also cause us to become foul, dirty, or unclean in the eyes of God. When this happens, you are then separated from God and are no longer under the covering and promises of God.

The Bible names the Promises of God—promises that will bless your life. Below are eleven of the more than three thousand Promises of God to us:

1. God promises to strengthen you.

"For this reason I bow my knees before the Father, from whom every family in heaven and on earth is named, that according to the riches of his glory he may grant you to be strengthened with power through his Spirit in your inner being" (Ephesians 3:14–16 (ESV)).

2. God promises to give you rest.

"Then Jesus said, 'Come to me, all of you who are weary and carry heavy burdens, and I will give you rest. Take my yoke upon you. Let me teach you, because I am humble and gentle at heart, and you will find rest for your souls. For my yoke is easy to bear, and the burden I give you is light'" (Matthew 11:28–30 (NLT)).

3. God promises to take care of all your needs.

"And this same God who takes care of me will supply all your needs from his glorious riches, which have been given to us in Christ Jesus" (Philippians 4:19 (NLT)).

4. God promises to answer your prayers.

"Ask, and it will be given to you; seek, and you will find; knock, and it will be opened to you" (Matthew 7:7 (ESV)).

5. God promises to work everything out for your good.

"And we know that God causes everything to

work together for the good of those who love God and are called according to his purpose for them" (Romans 8:28 (NLT)).

6. God promises to be with you

"I will not fail you or abandon you. This is my command—be strong and courageous! Do not be afraid or discouraged. For the Lord your God is with you wherever you go" (Joshua 1:5, 9 (NLT)).

7. God promises to protect you.

"This I declare about the LORD: He alone is my refuge, my place of safety; he is my God, and I trust him" (Psalm 91:2 (NLT)).

8. God promises freedom from sin.

"But if we confess our sins to him, he is faithful and just to forgive us our sins and to cleanse us from all wickedness" (1 John 1:9 (NLT)).

"So if the Son sets you free, you will be free indeed" (John 8:36 (ESV)).

9. God promises that nothing can separate you from Him.

"For I am sure that neither death nor life, nor angels nor rulers, nor things present nor things to come, nor powers, nor height nor depth, nor anything else in all creation, will be able to separate us from the love of God in Christ Jesus our Lord" (Romans 8:38–39 (ESV)).

10. God promises you everlasting life.

"For God so loved the world, that he gave his only Son, that whoever believes in him should not perish but have eternal life" (John 3:16 (ESV)).

11. God promises to never leave or forsake us.

"Be strong and courageous. Do not be afraid or terrified because of them, for the Lord your God goes with you; he will never leave you nor forsake you" (Deuteronomy 31:6 (NIV)).

Promise eleven is my favorite, because I feel it undergirds all the other promises. I encourage you to affirm daily these eleven promises by memorizing and meditating upon them. They will keep you confident no matter what's going on in your life. These promises have assured me that God is always with me and working things out for my good. In addition, these promises help me to stand in faith no matter how challenging life might be. I hold on to the hope that these promises give.

"For God so loved the world that he gave his one and only Son, that whoever believes in him shall not perish but have eternal life" (John 3:16 (ESV)).

"For all of God's promises have been fulfilled in Christ with a resounding "Yes!" And through Christ, our "Amen" (which means "Yes") ascends to God for his glory" (2 Corinthians 1:20 (NLT)).

Witchcraft is destructive: **"A man or woman who is a medium or spiritist among you must be put to death. You are to stone them; their blood will be on their own heads"** (Leviticus 20:27 (NIV)).

The reason God wants you to stay away from these things is that they will destroy you. If you practice witchcraft, it will taint you, pollute you, and if you allow it to continue in your life, it will ultimately destroy you. God took this very seriously and so should you. Consider how God dealt with those who practiced witchcraft.

"I will set my face against anyone who turns to mediums and spiritists to prostitute themselves by following them, and I will cut them off from their people" **(Leviticus 20:6 (NIV)).**

There are two facts about witchcraft that you may not be aware of that can potentially affect you. They include:

1. WITCHCRAFT CAN COME UPON YOU FROM HAVING A REBELLIOUS SPIRIT.

The Bible teaches us that rebellion is witchcraft: *"For rebellion is like the sin of divination, and arrogance like the evil of idolatry"* **(1 Samuel 15:23 (NIV)).**

The greatest example of witchcraft we see currently comes through rebellion. Remember, witchcraft is when you seek to manipulate through spiritual means. The spirit of rebellion is witchcraft because in essence, you are following another spirit to get revenge, hurt, or harm someone you feel have wronged you. Rebellion is also a strong desire to get what you want by any means necessary.

When you are engaged in rebellion, you are following your own spirit to pursue your own desires. It's extremely challenging for people to accept the facts given to us in 1 Samuel, that rebellion is a sin of divination. It's much easier to think that witchcraft comes from others casting spells on us than to accept that witchcraft can be caused by our choices.

The spirit of rebellion comes from having a spirit of unforgiveness. Forgiving is very difficult. Especially when someone you love hurts you.

We have all been hurt by the actions or words of others. It may have been a parent who constantly criticized you growing up or who rejected you, a friend who betrayed you, a coworker who sabotaged a project, or your partner had an affair. Or maybe you've had a traumatic experience, such as being physically or emotionally abused by someone close to you. These wounds can leave you with lasting feelings of anger and bitterness—even vengeance. But if you don't practice forgiveness, you might be the one who pays most dearly. By embracing forgiveness, you can also embrace peace, hope, gratitude, and joy. Consider how forgiveness can lead you down the path of physical, emotional, and spiritual well-being.

I also believe that other negative spirits can open the door or portal for witchcraft into our being and take over our spirits.

2. Witchcraft Dwells in Your Sinful Nature

Scripture tells us witchcraft can potentially live within your sinful nature. This means that although we are Christians, there is a part of us that could potentially be drawn to witchcraft, because our sinful nature still lives inside of us. In Galatians 5:19–21 (NIV), the Bible tells us, *"The acts of the flesh are obvious: sexual immorality, impurity and debauchery; idolatry and witchcraft; hatred, discord, jealousy, fits of rage, selfish ambition, dissensions, factions and envy; drunkenness, orgies, and the like. I warn you, as I did before, that those who live like this will not inherit the kingdom of God."*

Keep in mind, witchcraft is seeking assistance through spiritual means that don't include God. Often those who want to bypass seeking assistance from God do so because they don't want to live up to his standard. To receive God's help, you must do things God's way. When you don't want to do that, then you seek help from another source—which is a form of rebellion and is also witchcraft. If this is an act of sinful nature, then we must guard our hearts because we can all be susceptible to following these things.

YOU SHOULD
NOT PURSUE WITCHCRAFT

Many people have a desire to know about spiritual things, which makes sense because we are spiritual beings. When you seek spiritual advice from anyone, you must be extremely careful. This holds especially true today because there are so many self-proclaimed prophets. Many of those who claim to be prophets are often doing so for financial gain. They don't always give true words that they hear from God and give untrue or inaccurate words.

There is one more Scripture you should consider as we talk about this topic. Look at this verse in Isaiah: *"When someone tells you to consult mediums and spiritists, who whisper and mutter, should not a people inquire of their God? Why consult the dead on behalf of the living? Consult God's instruction and the testimony of warning. If anyone does not speak according to this word, they have no light of dawn"* **(Isaiah 8:19–20 (NIV)).**

The primary reason you should never seek after spiritists, mediums, sorcerers, or witches is that you have the Spirit of God living inside of you. When you need any type of assistance or answers, you can go directly to him. You don't have to run after these things which are destructive; you can consult your heavenly Father who has your best interests at heart.

Witchcraft is deceptive, dangerous, and deadly. God has warned us throughout the Bible to stay away from it. You should receive the warnings from God and strive to become filled with more and more of the Holy Spirit. This is not only the best help you will ever receive, but it is also the only spiritual assistance you will ever need.

Chapter Five

I Know
Witchcraft Is Real

"For rebellion is like the sin of divination, and arrogance like the evil of idolatry. Because you have rejected the word of the LORD, he has rejected you as king" (1 Samuel 15:23 (NIV)).

During my preteen and early teenage years, God was using me in a supernatural way to perform miracles, signs, and wonders in the lives of a lot of people. Churches and religious groups were inviting me to evangelize all over the country. In fact, I had so many engagements that I could not accept them all.

The Spirit of the Lord was genuinely upon me, and God was using me according to the words declared by Jesus in Luke 4:18–19 (NIV):

> *The Spirit of the Lord is on me,*
> *because he has anointed me*
> *to proclaim good news to the poor.*

He has sent me to proclaim freedom for the prisoners
    and recovery of sight for the blind,
to set the oppressed free,
    to proclaim the year of the Lord's favor.

The devil was beyond agitated; he was angry, outraged, and demented with madness, so he set out to destroy me. He wanted to stop the ministry path that the Lord had me on. If I was prevented from moving forward in the deliverance anointing that was upon my life, many in bondage of captivity would not be liberated. Countless numbers of people would miss their blessing of deliverance from the grip of Satan that held them bound. If Satan was able to bind me in a life of witchcraft, it would hamper the plan God had for my life.

Many adolescent preachers, male and female, often take on the spirit of witchcraft that tries and oftentimes succeeds in blocking us from carrying out the mission and purpose that God has for our lives—according to the Gospel of Luke 4, just as the devil tried to stop Jesus from living out his mission and purpose of healing and delivering the people with love, hope, and the Word of Truth.

The devil used my biological father as the stepping-stone to detour me off the path of ministry work God had me on. My father, by most standards, was a very successful man. He had a great job that paid very well. My father owned his house, our house, and several other rental properties. He also owned at least four cars. In addition, he had a wife and children.

It only took one of those occasional visits by my father to our house to cause me to alter the course of life. My father had been a man missing in action in the life of my siblings and me most of our childhood. However, the few times he would show up, he would exhibit a take-charge type of authority over everyone and everything in our household. This man, who gave no financial, emotional, or spiritual contributions to my mother nor any of his children, had the audacity to want us to respect him as the man of our household.

His mission of control was accomplished by his usage of physical, mental, and emotional abuse. Sometimes his words could be so severely harsh that they would cause me to shutter, run, and hide in shame and fear. The words hurt, but I must admit the beatings were extremely painful, cruel, harsh, and almost unbearable at times.

His abusiveness was especially aimed at me, because the devil (demonic) spirit in him could see the Christ spirit in me. In other words, the devil in him was trying to destroy the Christ in me! In addition, he also knew I was not afraid of him and that I truly hated him. My eyes would reflect the disdain, venom, acrimony, and more that I held in my heart for this man. The primary catalyst for the animosity I held for my father was rooted in the harsh manner in which he treated my mother, which included disrespect, rejection, physical and emotional anguish, as well as sexual abuse.

As he beat me, I would often think about our enslaved ancestors being beat by the white slave master. The slave master beat the slave because he was trying to beat the spirit of freedom out of the slave. My father, like the slave master, was trying to break the spirit of freedom, hope, peace, joy, and more of his wife and children in order to replace it with a spirit of fear, hopelessness, and intimidation. I was determined that I was not going to allow him to alter my spirit of being. Like a rebellious slave, I stood steadfast that he would not destroy my free will.

In spite of my resolve not to allow my father to control me, he still accomplished his mission, because I did change. I was no longer the man God had called me to be, but had become a monster. The Spirit of God within me was transformed into a spirit of hatred and rebellion. **The boy preacher became a little street thug!**

A spirit of rebellion had come into me and attached itself to me due to the hatred I had for my abusive father.

I rebelled by acting out against him and began fighting him back when he attacked my mother, my siblings, or me. After one of his vicious attacks, I plotted to kill my father. That night he would have died in his sleep had it not been for my mother stopping me.

The spirit of rebellion was now controlling me. It reached the point that I rebelled against almost every authority figure, especially males that I encountered (I will talk more about that later). At school, I would attack my teachers and principals with harsh words. On the street, I would curse the police, even fight them. I didn't fear going to jail or dying. I no longer went to church, but when the preacher tried to talk to or pray for me, they, too, would suffer the rage of my filthy words and rebellion.

According to *Dictionary.com*, rebellion is "open, organized, and armed resistance to one's government or ruler; resistance to defiance of any authority, control or tradition; the act of rebelling."

Rebellion is also one of the portals (doorways) that allows the spirit of witchcraft to attach itself to people. Witchcraft is a spirit of control. It controls us and causes us to act in ungodly ways. Once the witchcraft attachment takes place, the demonic spirit enters into your being, your body, mind, and spirit. You then lose control of your actions to do right or good, because witchcraft now controls you to do evil. Your life is out of control, and you seek to create chaos, division, confusion, and destruction in the lives of others. The Bible tells us in John 10:10 (NIV), ***"The thief* [devil] *comes to steal and kill and destroy; I* [Jesus] *have come that they may have life, and have it to the full."***

The spirit of rebellion and my rebelling opened me up to the demonic spirit called witchcraft. I became evil and did evil things—I broke the law. I became arrogant and would take revenge on those who rejected me and those I didn't like. A ruthless thug who sold drugs, pimped women, and would kill anyone who got in my way.

CHAPTER SIX

WITCHCRAFT
HAD A HOLD ON ME

"For rebellion is like the sin of divination, and arrogance like the evil of idolatry. Because you have rejected the word of the LORD, he has rejected you as king" (1 Samuel 15:23 (NIV)).

Due to the hatred I had for that abusive man, a spirit of rebellion had come into me and attached itself to me. The rebellion spirit that now possessed me had become a portal for witchcraft to enter into my mind, body and being. My being, character and who I was transformed into an evil person.

I rebelled by acting out against my father by attacking him with words when I saw him. One evening, after one of his vicious attacks on me, I plotted in my mind to kill my father. I knew his standard routine when he came to our house. He would beat one of us in the house, eat, and then go into my mother's bedroom with her and close the door.

My mother would come out of the bedroom once he had fallen asleep looking embarrassed, humiliated, and defeated. I also knew exactly where he always placed his pants in the bedroom—always on the same chair. Inside his pants pockets, there were always two items: a pocketful of money and a gun.

On this last evening of my final beating, I decided on how I was going to kill him and the satisfaction that I would feel from watching him die. It's interesting when I reflect back—I never thought about what would happen to me for killing this man! My mind was only focused on one thing: I wanted him to suffer, to die, and I wanted to bring an end to the anguish he caused my family.

While my mother was in the bedroom with him, I anxiously waited for her to come out. When she finally appeared, I quietly sneaked into the bedroom and closed the door. He was in a deep sleep, snoring. I looked at him with disgust and disdain in my eyes as I crept over to the chair that held his pants. I retrieved the revolver then moved toward the bed. As he slept, I stood over him, looking down on him, and cursed him for being so cruel to us.

Slowly, I lifted the gun and pointed it toward his head. Just as I was about to pull the trigger, I heard my mother's voice crying, "Don't do it, don't kill him! Put the gun down!" I was so focused on killing him I never heard the bedroom door open.

I put the gun down without pulling the trigger. I ran out of the house with anger and regret that I was not able to kill him. And I ran deeper into the street world of evil.

PART THREE

DING-DONG, THE WITCH IS DEAD

Chapter Seven

Power to Stop the Witch Possession

"Finally, be strong in the Lord and in his mighty power. Put on the full armor of God, so that you can take your stand against the devil's schemes" (Ephesians 6:10–11 (NIV)).

The Armor of God

Finally, be strong in the Lord and in his mighty power. Put on the full armor of God, so that you can take your stand against the devil's schemes. For our struggle is not against flesh and blood, but against the rulers, against the authorities, against the powers of this dark world and against the spiritual forces of evil in the heavenly realms. Therefore put on the full armor of God, so that when the day of evil comes, you may be able to stand your ground, and after you have done everything, to stand. Stand firm then, with the belt of truth buckled around your waist, with the *breastplate of righteousness in place, and with your feet fitted with the readiness that comes from the gospel of peace. In addition to all this, take up the shield of faith, with which you can extinguish all the flaming arrows of the evil one. Take the helmet of salvation and the sword of the Spirit, which is the word of God.*

And pray in the Spirit on all occasions with all kinds of prayers and requests. With this in mind, be alert and always keep on praying for all the Lord's people **(Ephesians 6:10–18 (NIV)).**

Ephesians 6:10–20 is believed to have been written by the Apostle Paul while he was guarded under house arrest by Roman soldiers. Paul's time of confinement allotted him ample time to study the gear of the soldiers. The whole armor of God is a metaphor of adorning ourselves daily with the protection of God.

It was during both of my jailhouse experiences that I reflected on my life and saw my errors and sins in life. During my rebellious season in life, I sold drugs and was arrested, but never served any prison time. The first time I was arrested I was about nineteen years old. As I reflected on my life, asking myself the question, "How did I get here?" I started seeking God in prayer and God started drawing closer to me. With the presence of God near me, I asked God to forgive me for running away from him and to forgive me for all of my sins. A sense of peace and of hope came over me.

I told God that when I got out of jail, I was going to lead a new life and once again serve him. It was also my thought that I needed to live in a new environment away from Miami. My cousin in Los

Angeles said I could come to live with him to get a fresh start on life. It took me almost a week on many buses to get to Los Angeles from Miami. I was excited about my season of new beginnings.

The six months or so went extremely well. I immediately got a job working at a fast-food restaurant. It was a great surprise to me that the pay in Los Angeles was a lot more than what I would be paid in Miami. The more I became familiar with Los Angeles, the less time I spent with God. The less time I spent with God, the more challenging things got in my life, especially with my roommate.

He started selling drugs! The very thing I was running from was in the house with me. But I continued working and saving money. One day, I came home and discovered that all the money I had saved—almost two thousand dollars—was gone! My cousin had stolen it to buy more drugs to use and sell. We fought verbally and physically; the police were called. I was told to leave the apartment.

And just like that I was homeless! One of my coworkers' family allowed me to temporarily live with them. It didn't take me long to get an apartment through a program that provided shelter for the homeless and food stamps. I was still working and once again doing okay, so I once again stopped seeking God's face. When the voucher for my apartment ran out, I was once again homeless.

This time, I moved in with a woman I didn't like just to have some place to live. Her brothers harassed me about joining their gang. When I would not join their gang, they beat me badly and kicked me out of her apartment. Yet again, I was homeless—no place to go and in severe pain after getting my butt kicked. At that moment, I decided to go home.

I called home and asked my mother for bus fare. She said she didn't have it but would ask my father. Of course, that man, who had never done anything for me, said no! He then told me to get home the best way I could. With those words, a rage of anger rose in me. His words called that spirit of rebellion, witchcraft, back to life.

Without his help, I made it home. My mother borrowed money to buy me a bus ticket home. My bus ride home was completely different from the one to Los Angeles. I completely forgot about praying, but concentrated on how I never wanted to be in this type of predicament again—of not having money or having my father or anyone else saying no to me if I asked them for money. Nor did I want my mother to have to ask anyone for money.

The long ride home stirred up more and more anger in me. I made two decisions on that long journey to Miami: I would sell drugs to make money, and I vowed, again, that I would kill my father. I arrived home with hatred in my heart and a desire to be a ruthless, drug-selling street thug.

That's exactly who I became: a cold-hearted, uncaring, and no-compassion-for-anyone dope dealer. I did not mind beating, shooting, stabbing, and if necessary, killing anyone who got in my way. As much as I hated and despised my father's ways, I had actually become my father. After several years of living my life in this manner, I was arrested and jailed for selling drugs.

Like the Apostle Paul my jail experience gave me lots of time to reflect over my life and the things I saw in my new surroundings As I reflected over my life, I started feeling guilty about the horrible things I had done to so many people. In addition, I also felt bad that I was not fulfilling God's purpose for my life. I repented to God about all my sinful wrongs. I even asked God to teach me how to forgive my father—and God did just what I asked. With all my heart, I wanted the God I knew as a boy to come back to me. The more I sought God, the more I felt the presence of God, and I began to feel the change occurring in my life.

God opened my eyes to see the needs of the people around me, my fellow inmates, and the guards. It became about others and not just about me. God used me to witness to others—praying, preaching, and prophesying.

As much and often as I could, I prayed, sought God's face, read my Bible, and put on the whole armor of God according to Ephesians 6:10–20. I would actually visualize myself putting on the whole armor of God.

"And the peace of God, which passeth all understanding, shall keep your hearts and minds through Christ Jesus" **(Philippians 4:7 (KJV))**. Although I was in jail, I was in total peace with God, my family, myself, and my circumstance. Like the old hymn, "It Is Well with My Soul," I decided that whatever my plight (prison sentencing), it was well with my soul—because this time, I truly wanted to serve God.

The first time I went before the judge, he offered me a thirty-year plea deal. I said no, I would take my chance at a trial. The second time I went before the judge, he offered me a twenty-year sentence. I continued praying, asking God for a miracle and trusting that God would work things out for me. The third time I went before the judge, he threw out the charges against me.

I have never stopped praising God for my miracle, forgiving me, using me, and blessing me!

Chapter Eight

Ring the Bell: Ding-Dong, the Witch Is Dead

"The thief comes only to steal and kill and destroy; I have come that they may have life, and have it to the full" (John 10:10 (NIV)).

Ding-Dong, the Witch Is Dead! That was my first and last time in jail and the witch in me has never shown up again, because daily I pray, seek God's face, and put on the whole armor of God.

It was completely evident that the witch was dead when my father was on his deathbed and I prayed for him. When I looked at him in his casket, I no longer felt any hatred, just pity. I had forgiven him, so there was no longer a rebellious spirit in me. With God's help, I had closed the portal for witchcraft forever.

Yet every day I put on the whole armor of God to

keep any new portals from opening. I suggest that in order for you to protect yourself from witchcraft, you also should put on the whole armor of God as listed in Ephesian 6:10–20.

At the end of all the fairy tales and children's books the witch dies. In *The Princess and the Frog*, the frog became a prince and the pretty girl a princess. In *The Wizard of Oz*, all the townspeople whose lives had been terrorized by the Wicked Witch of the West danced and sang a song that the witch was dead.

God has elevated me from being a ruthless, drug-selling street thug to being a Prophet, Overseer, and now, a Bishop for God! There is not a day that goes by that I don't praise God and give God the Glory, because I, too, can sing with authority and might, ***Ding-Dong, the Witch Is Dead!***

About the Author

I am a Prophet, an Overseer, and Bishop—a man the Lord spoke to—a prophetic voice for the nation. To me, the only belief is to believe in the Lord for everyone's miracles, signs, and wonders.